The Divorce Workbook

A Guide for Kids and Families

Sally Blakeslee Ives, Ph.D.
David Fassler, M.D.
Michele Lash, M.Ed., A.T.R.

Waterfront Books
85 Crescent Road
Burlington, Vermont 05401

ISBN: 0-914525-05-0 (paperback)

Twelvth Printing, March 1999

Designed and produced by Robinson Book Associates
Printed in the United States by Daamen, Inc.

Contents

On Using This Book

Separation and divorce are traumatic events for families. The changes and feelings can be very confusing for both adults and children. We wrote this book to help children express, explore, and understand some of the many emotions triggered by the separation and divorce process. Some of these thoughts and reactions may be unpleasant or upsetting. As caring adults, we can help by acknowledging and understanding such responses. When using this book, it is important to be flexible. Some children may want to complete the book in one sitting, while others may wish to explore a section at a time as issues or concerns arise. Used in a supportive environment, **The Divorce Workbook** can facilitate honest and open communication between adults and children at a difficult time.

Suggestions for Parents

1. Explain to the child that this is a different kind of book, one in which he or she can share feelings and thoughts through both drawings and words. Unlike school books or library books, this is a book in which to write and draw.

2. Young children may need to have the book read aloud. For some, it may be best to read the book in several sittings.

3. Let the child know that he or she can have a safe place in which to store the book. Make sure the child has access to the book.

4. Let the child work on the book at his or her own pace, and choose the order in which to complete the chapters. Children will use the book in many different ways.

5. Make sure the child has access to writing and drawing materials.

6. If you are reading the book with a child, pick a quiet time and a private place. This is a time to concentrate on the child and his or her feelings.

7. Be accepting and non-judgmental. Let the child know that there are no right or wrong answers or feelings. Accept the child's emotions as valid and important.

8. Some children may wish to read the book without writing or drawing. They may decide to add their own thoughts, comments and artwork at a later time.

9. When working through the "Legal Stuff" section, use it as an opportunity to help the child understand the terms pertaining to his or her own family situation. This can be an opportunity to correct misunderstandings.

10. When the child wants to stop working on the book, respect his or her wishes. You can always return to it at a later point.

11. Parents, teachers and other caring adults may also find the book useful to help them understand the child's perspective in a changing family situation.

Suggestions for Counselors

Individual Therapy:

1. **The Divorce Workbook** may be used in the context of individual therapy to enhance the child's expression of his or her thoughts and feelings. Reading the book can also be supportive and reassuring as the child realizes that his or her experiences are similar to those of other children.

2. Work through the chapters, paying particular attention to the sections most pertinent to the child's situation and emotional status.

3. **The Divorce Workbook** is a therapeutic tool, which can be used in conjunction with other expressive techniques such as play, art, music, drama and movement.

Group Therapy:

1. **The Divorce Workbook** can be used as the framework for short-term therapeutic groups.

2. Group sessions can be organized around particular chapters or themes in the book.

3. In the group setting, opportunities can be provided for children to complete the drawing and writing activities suggested in the book.

4. Drawings, stories, poems, and other creative expressions generated by the group of children can be collated and copied for group members.

Suggestions for Teachers

1. When a class contains a number of children from separated or divorced families, sharing the book with the entire group can help children begin to talk about their individual situations with their peers.

2. It is best not to identify aloud the children in the class from divorced families, but rather let the identification come spontaneously from the children themselves.

3. Children should not be graded or judged on the activities contained in the book.

4. This book may elicit strong emotions from some children. Use of the book may help identify children who should be referred to the school guidance counselor.

5. **The Divorce Workbook** can also be used individually, either by a teacher with the permission of the child's parent, or by recommending the book to a parent for use at home.

Suggestions for Librarians

1. **The Divorce Workbook** may be particularly useful for children who do not like to read, or those with a short attention span. The hands-on, interactive format serves to personalize the experience and engage the child.

2. The librarian can help children explore the different ways they might use the book — on their own, with a parent, or with another adult friend or professional.

3. **The Divorce Workbook** may present a dilemma for librarians since children are not traditionally permitted to write or draw in library books. In the library setting, the book can be used as a reference or with adult supervision.

Also available from the same authors:

**Changing Families:
A Guide for Kids and Grown-ups**
Waterfront Books, 1988

and

**My Kind of Family:
A Book for Kids in Single-Parent Homes**
Waterfront Books, 1990

Acknowledgments

Special thanks to:

Joan Bernheimer, Ph.D.
Mary Carrier, M.S.W.
Charles B. Cerasoli, MAT, CAS
Howard Graman, M.D.
Sandra Kaler, R.N., M.S.
Michael Lash
Betsy Lawrence, A.C.S.W.
Gloria Lyman
Justin Lyman

Roger Moyer
Kathi Newburger, M.Ed., A.T.R.
Suzanne Niquette
Ronald C. Schmucker, J.D.
Cathy Simonson, M.Ed.
Marga Sproul, M.D.
Irm Wessel, A.C.S.W.
Morris Wessel, M.D.
Betsey, Nathaniel, Heather & Julie

and the children at the Malletts Bay School in Colchester, Vermont.

CHAPTER 1

Marriage

People have been getting married for thousands of years. They've also been getting divorced for almost as long.

Why do people get married? Kids have lots of ideas.

THEY LOVE AND CARE FOR EACH other.
THEY THINK THEY WANT TO STAY
TogeTher Forever.
It's not so lonely if you are with SomeBody you like.
They want to start a Family.

People get married because they love each other.

Why do you think people get married?

Why do you think people have kids?

There are many different kinds of families.

13

Draw your family here.

Families go through many changes. Some of them feel good, and some of them may feel scary and bad. Sometimes things become so bad that parents begin to think about separating.

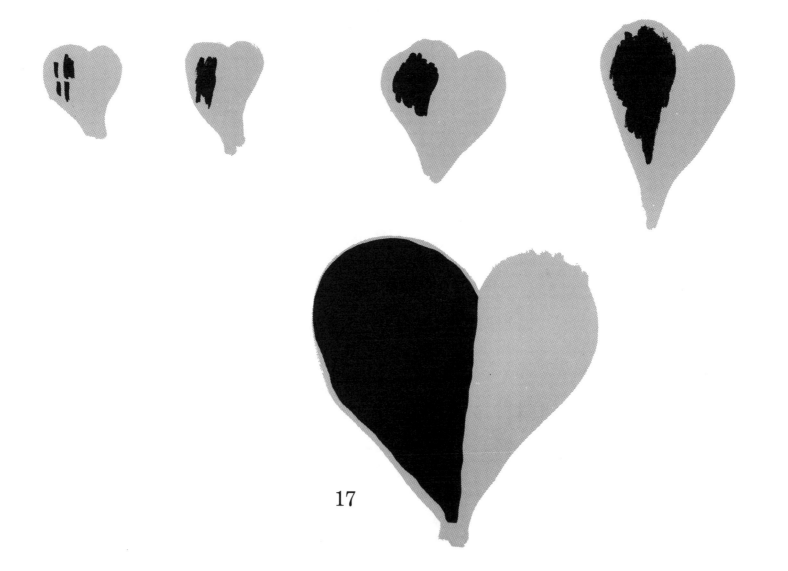

CHAPTER 2

Separation

A separation is when parents decide to live apart from each other and figure out what to do about their marriage.

Dont think its the end of the world
And Don't even think it's your fault because it isn't.
Sometimes the parents might think thay are right for each other
But once they are married for awhile they want to make changes
Like they don't want to be together any more. And they are
going in different directions.

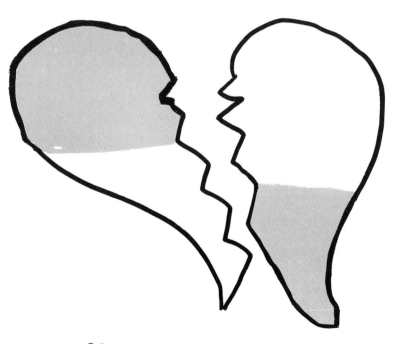

Draw a separation here.

Why did my parents even get married? Why do I have go through with this?

Sometimes a separation is a hard thing to talk about. It's not always easy to tell people that your mom and dad are not living together.

Don't be afraid to tell your friends it might be better for you later on!

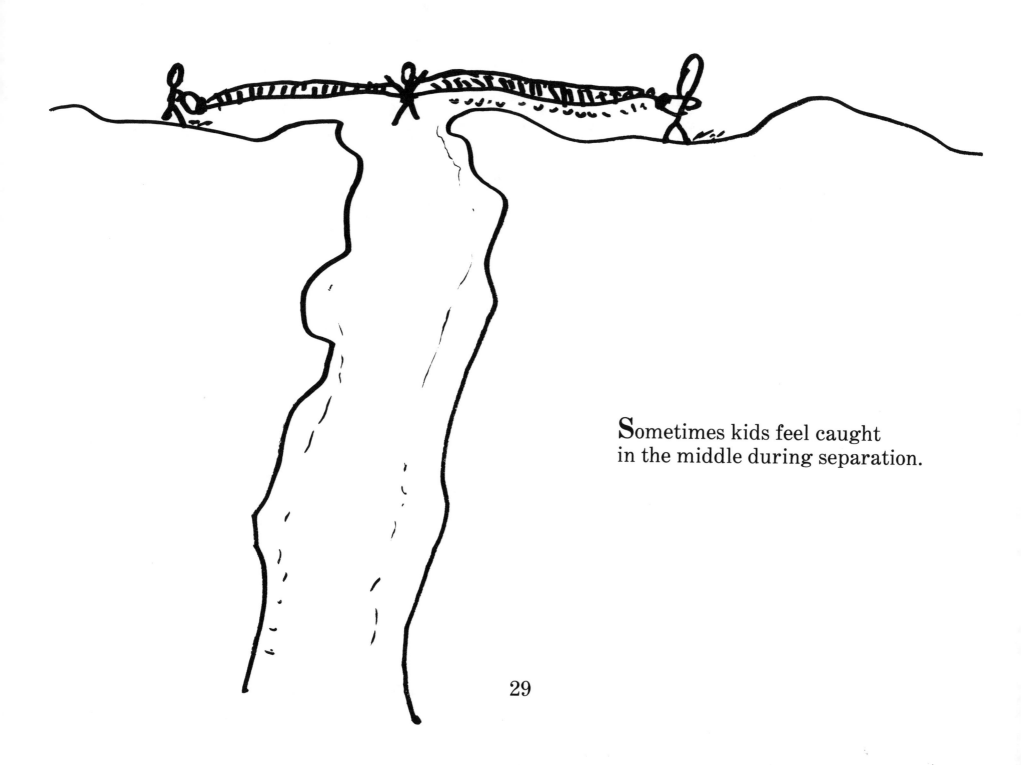

Sometimes kids feel caught
in the middle during separation.

29

Don't hope for your parents to get back together because most of the time they won't.

Usually kids want their parents to stay together. But sometimes things feel so bad that a child wishes parents would separate.

Did you ever feel that way?

Strange as it might seem, sometimes things are better for a family when the parents decide to separate.

My parents fought all the time. I was scared. Once the police had to come.

When parents separate, kids may wind up living in a new place.

Did you have to move?

Did you have to change schools?

A separation can be long or short. It can even go on for years. During the separation, parents may decide to get back together. Or, they may decide it would be best for everyone in the family if they divorce. Sometimes they have problems deciding what to do.

CHAPTER 3

Divorce

A divorce is when two people decide they no longer want to be married. They can't live together happily anymore. They decide to stop being husband and wife. They continue as parents to their children.

One thing never changes. Your mother will always be your mother, and your father will always be your father. You still have a family when your parents get divorced.

Divorce is often hard to accept but
its taken place. There is nothing you can
do to stop it.
The reason for divorce is, your parents don't
think They were right adout marriage and
don't think they should stay together.

Draw a picture of divorce.

Some kids think that the divorce happened because of them doing something wrong and say "I promise I'll never be bad again!" But it really isn't your fault. Sometimes your parents just can't get along.

My parents fought about the mess I made.

Barbie

Bear

TOYS

car

doll

The mess.

Lots of kids think they caused the divorce. They feel it's their fault. Maybe they did something bad or wrong. If they were better behaved, maybe the divorce would not have happened.

Kids cannot cause a divorce. They also cannot keep a mom and dad together. Divorce, like marriage, is between adults only.

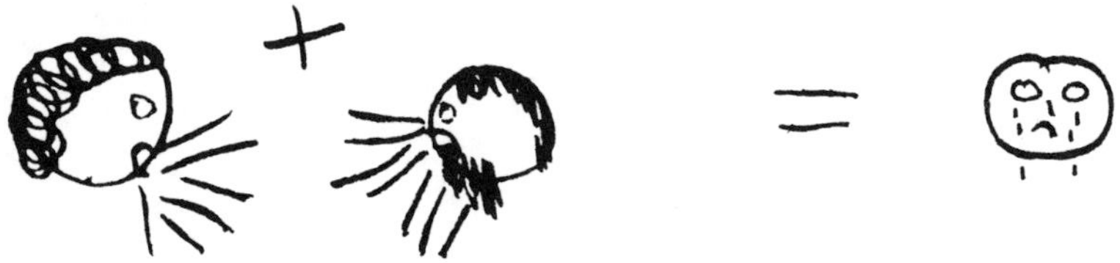

DON'T Blame

IT ON yourself!!

53

CHAPTER 4

Legal Stuff

When two adults decide to divorce, at least one of them has to go to a courtroom to talk to a judge. The judge helps figure out the rules for the divorce. The judge makes the divorce official by having a document—a paper—written out. The paper says things about visiting, living with, and caring for the children. It says the adults are no longer married but continue to be parents.

Sometimes Judges are scary and look like monsters because they wear long black robes. It's kind of their uniform. They're really not scary and they want to help you.

59

Sometimes a child must go to court to talk about the family and his or her feelings. The judge wants to know what it's like to be a child in the family, so he or she can make fair decisions. That's the judge's job and responsibility.

Lawyers are people who help parents understand the laws about divorce. Each parent may have his or her own lawyer. Sometimes lawyers go to court and help the parents talk to the judge.

The children in a divorce may have their own lawyer or advocate. This is a special person who helps the judge figure out what is best for the children.

Your lawyer is a person who stands up for you in court.

It's boring just listening to the lawyers. It's hard to keep a straight face and still yawn!

**What do you think a courtroom looks like?
Draw a picture here.**

Legal stuff can be pretty confusing. Here are some new words and what they mean:

Custody is the decision about who is in charge and responsible for the children. This includes deciding where the children will live and go to school. Parents often work together to make these kinds of important decisions, but the person who has custody has the final say.

Joint Custody is when both parents agree that they will share in all the responsibilities and decisions about the children.

Child Support is the money one parent gives to the other to help pay for the things the children need.

Divorce Mediation is when parents work out the rules for their divorce with the help of a counselor called a mediator. The mediator listens to both sides and helps the parents reach an agreement. The judge still has to make the agreement official.

Visitation Arrangements are the rules about when, where, and how often the children will see or stay with each parent. There are many different kinds of arrangements.

you get to visit and stay over and stuff
I visit my dad for the whole summer

I visit my mom every weekend.

My dad and I go and do things

every Wednesday.

Dad's house ↙

Moms house ↙

15 miles

age 10

CHAPTER 5

Feelings

When parents get separated and divorced, kids naturally have lots of different feelings.

Pick some words that tell how you feel. Add any others you want.

• angry	• ignored	• embarrassed
• trapped	• happy	• nervous
• scared	• sad	• relieved
• confused	• lonely	• safe
• worried	• guilty	• uncertain
_____	_____	_____
_____	_____	_____

What's going to happen to me?

Draw a picture of a feeling here.

88

When parents get divorced, it feels really sad. Sometimes you even feel like running away.

Divorce Feels Awful, like your
Parents are shutting you down and not
Loving You, Sometimes they get so upset and
yell And scream at you. But other times
they say they love you and it makes you
Feel good. But when they tell you they're getting
Divorced it feels like your heart shatters.

Most kids feel angry about divorce.

93

After my parents got divorced, my mom had to go to work to earn more money. We still can't buy all the things we used to.

When my parents got divorced I had lots of tummy aches.

99

It makes me feel funny to do things with Dad & his new Girlfriend

103

CHAPTER 6

Helping Yourself

When a divorce happens, it is important to take care of yourself. One way to help yourself is to have a special person, other than your parents, to talk to. Special people can be sisters, brothers, aunts, uncles, grandparents, friends, neighbors, teachers, counselors, ministers, priests, rabbis . . . .

Can you think of anyone else?

The psychologist helps you to sort out your feelings.

When parents are separating or divorcing, many children find special things or places that help them get through the rough times.

Draw a picture of yourself, in a special place or with a special thing.

Sometimes a favorite pet can help you get through your parent's divorce.

Do you have a favorite pet? Draw a picture of your pet.

Even while a divorce is happening, it's O.K. and important to have fun.

Draw yourself having fun.

Draw a picture of things you like to do with your mom.

Show what you like to do with your dad.

Kids have lots of good ideas that could help.

Talk to someone else whose family has been through divorce.

A way to get out your feelings
is: To punch your pillow,
 If you can you should even
 go in your room, shut
 the door and cry or
 Scream.

But you shouldn't punch
People.

IF You Are having trouble
with your Parents Because
your Parents are separated
Or divorced you should go and
talk to some one a bout the
Problems.

When you are Really mad:

1. Go play, Don't think of it.
2. Don't think of Divorce.
3. Don't Blame it on your self.
4. Never Bring it out on your Sister or Brother.

Don't be afraid to cry. Somtimes crying makes you feel better. Even parents need to cry sometimes!

If your parents are getting divorced and they are "dragging it out" talk to them. Let them know how you feel. Tell them you want it over. Because the parent moving out usually doesn't want to, the above situation happens too often. You can always talk to parents. Bear that in mind. You can also talk to siblings, or step parents, & friends.

DID you know that 50% of all marriges that start end in Divorce? If Your parents are divorced, that Statistic probably doesn't exactly Comfort You but it lets you know:

YoU
Are
Not
Alone.

Kids also have lots of ideas for their parents about divorce.

- Parents should stop fighting once the papers are signed. That means it's over. Finished! No more!

- They should follow the rules.

- Parents should tell kids what's going on. We need to know!

- Don't put kids in the middle. It's not our fault.

- Don't use me as a messenger!

- Don't tell me bad things about Daddy.

- Try to be nice to each other.

- If you date, be careful of your children's feelings.

- Don't keep buying me toys. It doesn't make me feel better.

- Don't fight about money.

What would <u>you</u> like <u>your</u> parents to know?

These pages are for you to make up stories or poems or draw any other pictures you'd like.

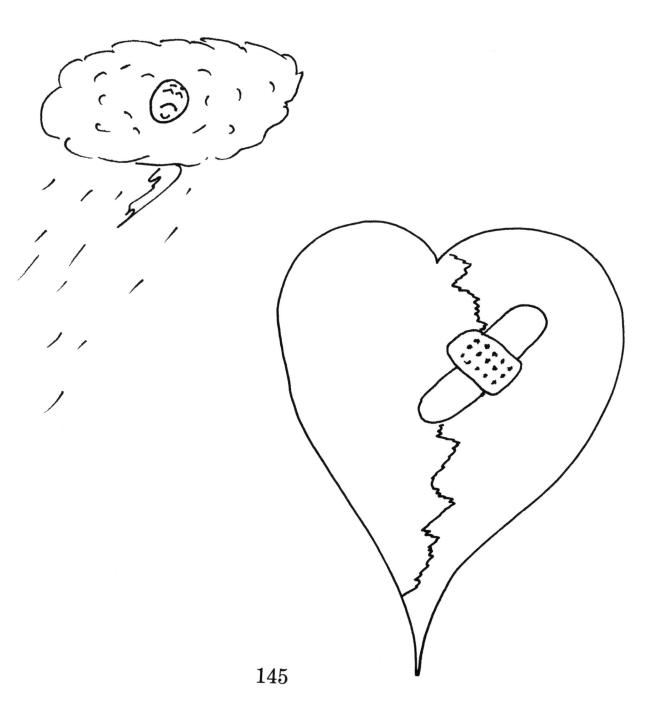

145

About the Authors

Sally (Blakeslee Ives) Loughridge is a child psychologist practicing in Burlington, Vermont. She received her Ph.D. from the Department of Human Development and Family Studies at Cornell University. A clinical associate professor of psychiatry at the University of Vermont, Dr. Loughridge is also a nationally certified school psychologist (NCSP) and listed in the National Register of Health Service Providers in Psychology.

David Fassler is a child psychiatrist practicing in Burlington, Vermont. A graduate of the Yale University School of Medicine, Dr. Fassler received his training in adult psychiatry at the University of Vermont, and in child psychiatry at the Cambridge Hospital, Harvard Medical School. He is currently a clinical assistant professor and the director of continuing education in the Department of Psychiatry at the University of Vermont, and an instructor in psychiatry at Cambridge Hospital, Harvard Medical School.

Michele Lash received her M.Ed. in expressive art therapies from Lesley College. She is currently affiliated with the Graduate Art Therapy Program at Vermont College. A registered art therapist and psychoeducational consultant, she is in private practice in Essex Junction, Vermont.

WHAT'S A VIRUS, ANYWAY?
The Kids' Book About AIDS
David Fassler, M.D. & Kelly McQueen

AIDS can be a difficult subject to discuss with young children. However, children hear a lot about the disease at a very early age. *What's a Virus, Anyway?* is a simple introduction to help adults talk with children. It provides basic information in a manner appropriate for 4-10 year olds.

"… that people with AIDS are just like everyone else makes this book particularly distinctive." — *Booklist*

Also, now a new Spanish edition:
¿QUE ES UN VIRUS?
Un Libro Para Niños Sobre el SIDA

$8.95 paper, $12.95 plastic comb spiral
Ages 4-10. 70 pages. Illustrated by children

THE DIVORCE WORKBOOK
A Guide for Kids and Families
Sally B. Ives, Ph.D., David Fassler, M.D., and Michelle Lash, M.Ed., A.T.R.

The volume takes children by the hand from marriage through separation, divorce and 'legal stuff' which defines such terms as custody, child support, divorce mediation, and visitation. It also devotes considerable attention to the emotional aftermath of divorce."

— **Nadine Brozan**, *New York Times*

$12.95 paper, $16.95 plastic comb spiral,
160 pages, illustrated by children. Ages 4-12

CHANGING FAMILIES
A Guide for Kids and Grown-ups
David Fassler, M.D., Michelle Lash, M.Ed., A.T.R. and Sally B. Ives, Ph.D.

This book helps children cope with the emotional confusion of being in a changing family. Divorce, remarriage, new surroundings, and new relatives are a few of the changes presented for discussion here.

"Many children of divorce openly or secretly hope that their biological parents will reunite. The new marriage shatters that illusion." —**David Fassler**, *during interview with Lawrence Kutner, in "Parent & Child," New York Times*

$14.95 paper, $18.95 plastic comb spiral
192 pages,illustrated by children. Ages 4-12

COMING TO AMERICA
The Kids' Book about Immigration
David Fassler, M.D. and Kimberly Danforth, M.A.

Many refugee children have experienced war, desperate circumstances, or natural disasters. Written and drawn with the help of children between the ages of 5 and 12, *Coming to America* can facilitate open and honest discussion about a child's immigration experience.

"It has a genuine voice which children and families will find comforting." —**Caroline Linse**, *Ministry of Education, Riga, Latvia*

$12.95 paper, $16.95 plastic comb spiral
160 pages, illustrated by children. Ages 5-12

"MY DAD'S *Definitely* NOT A DRUNK!"
Elisa Lynn Carbone

A realistic and sensitive portrayal of family dynamics in an alcoholic's home…. Few books for this age group effectively convey the experiences of children in this situation without villainizing the parent. Carbone not only does the job nicely, but also provides good information in the process."

—*School Library Journal, Fall 1992*

$7.95 paper, $11.95 hardcover
100 pages. Grades 6-9.

WATERFRONT BOOKS
85 Crescent Road, Burlington, VT 05401
Order toll-free: 1-800-639-6063

MY KIND OF FAMILY
A Book for Kids in Single-Parent Homes
Michelle Lash, M.Ed., Sally Ives Loughridge, Ph.D., and David Fassler, M.D.

Helps children express, explore and understand some of the special issues and feelings associated with living in a single-parent home.

$14.95 paper, $18.95 plastic comb spiral
208 pages, illustrated by children. Ages 4-12

JOSH
A Boy with Dyslexia
Caroline Janover

An adventure story for kids with a section of resources and facts about learning disabilities.

*"In **Josh**, Caroline Janover has taken me into the mind and heart of **A Boy with Dyslexia**. We share his fears, tragedies, and triumphs. Must reading for all families who struggle with dyslexia."* —**Mary MacCracken**, *educational therapist and author of **Lovey, Turnabout Children**, and **Circle of Children***

$7.95 paper, $11.95 hardcover
100 pages, 15 illustrations. Ages 8-12

LUKE HAS ASTHMA, TOO
Alison Rogers
Illustrated by Michael Middleton

The story shows that asthma can be managed in a calm fashion. For the more than two million families who have children with asthma, this is an important message." — **Thomas F. Plaut, M.D.,** *author of **Children with Asthma: A Manual for Parents***

$6.95 paper
32 pages, illustrated. Ages 3-7

LET'S TALK TRASH
The Kids' Book About Recycling
Kelly McQueen and David Fassler, M.D.

Never has 'talking trash' been so much fun! This book takes a refreshing look at a tough problem. I hope kids will share this book with their parents so that we all understand why it's important to protect our beautiful environment."

—**Madeleine M. Kunin**, *Governor of Vermont*

$14.95 paper, $18.95 plastic comb spiral
168 pages, illustrated by children. Ages 4-10